LORD GIVE ME A
REPENTANT
HEART

Thomas LeBlanc

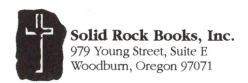

Solid Rock Books, Inc.
979 Young Street, Suite E
Woodburn, Oregon 97071

First Printing

Published by

Solid Rock Books, Inc.
979 Young Street, Suite E
Woodburn, Oregon 97071

ISBN 187-911-2221

Printed in the United States of America.

DEDICATION

This booklet is dedicated to the following:

The high school evangelism team at
Country Christian School in Molalla, Oregon.
They are examples of young people
who are on fire for God — who are anxious
to share His Word in any and every way possible.

and

The evangelism team at Northwest College
in Kirkland, Washington. They demonstrated
to me the meaning of Psalm 126:5-6,

"They that sow in tears shall reap in joy.
He that goeth forth and weepeth,
bearing precious seed, shall doubtless
come again with rejoicing,
bringing his sheaves with him."

and

To evangelist Dwight Kinman, who is like a
spiritual father to me. He has demonstrated the
meaning and importance of John 3:30,

"He (Jesus) must increase, but I must decrease."

TABLE OF CONTENTS

PREFACE

I think the man who inspired me the most in writing this booklet was Ray Comfort. His book *Hell's Best Kept Secret* helped me to realize that repentance is the means by which God brings sinners to salvation. Then one day, as I was meditating on Acts 3:19, I realized that repentance is not only for lost sinners but also for saved sinners like me. The Lord started showing me that repentance must be a daily attitude of mind. So I started asking the Lord for a repentant heart.

Soon I noticed that my prayer life was becoming more alive. In fact, praying seemed to be transforming from an obligation into an addiction. One morning, while I was engaged in intense prayer, I felt like the Holy Spirit was whispering a promise to my heart. This "Harvest Promise" is found in the last chapter of this booklet. It was a very encouraging word that gave me hope that America can turn back to God before it is too late.

Then the Lord started to place a vision of revival in my heart. It was an image of something I had never heard of or read about. In my mind I could see entire congregations under the conviction of the Holy Spirit. The people were bowed down in repentance and were weeping because of their sins against God. The sight was so unbelievable and unheard of to me that I was reluctant to tell anyone about it. I finally told two pastors, one of which was Dwight Kinman.

A couple of weeks later Pastor Kinman gave me the book *By My Spirit*, by Jonathan Goforth, the great missionary to China. I was thrilled as I read, because he described entire congregations weeping before the Lord in repentance — the same as I had seen. Just as I finished reading Goforth's book, Pastor Kinman put me in touch with Mary Goforth Moynan, the last living daughter of Jonathan Goforth. Pastor Kinman knew the family and wrote the foreword to Jonathan Goforth's book.

I called Mary Goforth Moynan to talk with her. She said she spent seventeen years on the missionary field with her father. I asked her about the mass repentance that I read about in her father's book. She said it was a very common occurrence when her father ministered. "In fact," she said, "My father would be very disappointed and even heart-broken if such a breakthrough did not happen after a couple of meetings."

Jonathan Goforth knew that when the Holy Spirit and conviction fell upon the people they would be revived. He knew that they would be changed and would be a catalyst of change for many others. It grieved him when this did not happen.

Think of how much Jesus is grieved when we do not allow Him to fully work in our lives. He wants to do more for us and through us than we are willing to allow Him to do. And this breaks His heart because He loves us. Sometimes during intense times of prayer, Christians can sense His broken heart and His grief.

My prayer is that we, as the representatives and body of Christ, will allow Jesus to mold us into the vessels He longs for us to become. Because only then can He empower us to accomplish the seemingly impossible tasks we face in our world today.

Introduction

The times in which we live are making it increasingly more difficult to serve God. The world has many enticements that tug on our hearts and compete for our love. Often our love for the world is greater than our love for the Father. Oh, we know the god of this world blinds the minds of unbelievers, but we fail to realize that he can also hide certain truths from our eyes. The enemy of our soul is using every strategy in his power to take us captive to do his will. As a result, many of God's people are prisoners to thoughts, habits and lifestyles that do not glorify Him.

If there ever was a time when God's people needed to be strong, it is today. A standard needs to be raised up in a land that despises standards. Godly living needs to be demonstrated in a nation that seeks to abolish all knowledge of God. And God's holiness needs to be demonstrated in a nation that does not know the difference between right and wrong. But we can not do this in our own strength. We can not accomplish this in our own power. We need to be in touch with the One who can make a difference. We need to be in a position

where His love, His compassion, His wisdom and
all of His power can readily flow through us. We
must grow so close to Jesus that we can sense how
He feels, what brings Him joy and what grieves His
heart.

How can we accomplish this? The answer is
interwoven throughout Scripture. God reveals that
the answer lies in His people developing repentant
hearts. Hearts that are sensitive to the convicting
voice of the Holy Spirit. Hearts that are eager to
repent and turn away from anything that builds
walls between them and God. Hearts that are
moldable in the Potter's hands on a daily basis.

Scripture reveals that a repentant heart can break
down the barriers that separate us from God and
from our fellow man. God also reveals in His Word
that the repentant heart is the key to revival.
Revival is an individual and personal experience.
But as the people of God are revived, one by one,
the church, as a whole, can experience revival. If
we are to see a change in the moral climate in our
country, we must first see a change in the moral
climate of God's people. God's people are clearly
the ones who have within their grasp the power to
change the nation. That is why God said,

> If my people, which are called by my name,
> shall humble themselves, and pray, and seek
> my face, and turn from their wicked ways
> [repentance]: then will I hear from heaven, and
> will forgive their sin, and will heal their land (2
> Chronicles 7:14.).

God has always judged sin. Yet I believe we
have set before us a narrow window of opportunity.

If we, as the church of the living God, will humble ourselves and seek Him with all of our hearts, He will bring forth revival in our individual lives and in our land. But we must respond to His call for repentance. And we must do it now while there is still time. Will the much-needed wave of revival break forth upon our land? Only if a wave of true repentance comes first. For God has promised to REVIVE those with repentant hearts (Isaiah 57:15.)

Two

Voices that call for Repentance

Throughout the ages and throughout Scripture God has called for repentance. The following are some of the voices He used:

Ezekiel
Therefore say unto the house of Israel, Thus saith the Lord GOD; REPENT, and turn yourselves from your idols; and turn away your faces from all your abominations (Ezekiel 14:6).

Therefore I will judge you, O house of Israel, every one according to his ways, saith the Lord GOD. REPENT, and turn yourselves from all your transgressions; so iniquity shall not be your ruin (Ezekiel 18:30).

John the Baptist
In those days came John the Baptist, preaching in the wilderness of Judaea, And saying, "REPENT ye: for the kingdom of heaven is at hand" (Matthew 3:1-2).

Jesus

From that time Jesus began to preach, and to say, "REPENT . . . for the kingdom of heaven is at hand" (Matthew 4:17).

And Jesus said to the Christians in five of the seven churches of Revelation, "REPENT" (Revelation chapters 2-3).

And Jesus said that REPENTANCE AND REMISSION OF SINS should be preached in His name among all nations, beginning at Jerusalem (Luke 24:47).

The Disciples

And they went out, and preached that men should REPENT (Mark 6:12).

Peter

Then Peter said unto them, "REPENT, and be baptized every one of you in the name of Jesus Christ for the remission of sins, and ye shall receive the gift of the Holy Ghost" (Acts 2:38).

God the Father

In the past God overlooked such ignorance, but now HE COMMANDS ALL PEOPLE EVERYWHERE TO REPENT (Acts 17:30 NIV).

Why such a clear and persistent call for repentance? One could determine by the frequency and intensity of God's call that repentance is a vital issue. So let us take a look at the anatomy of repentance. In this way, we can better understand the nature of true repentance.

Three

The Anatomy of Repentance

Rocky soil cannot bear fruit. Have you ever tried to plant seeds in a rocky garden with crusty hard soil? It is difficult to even dig deep enough to plant the seeds. And those seeds that do sprout will have very little chance of maturing and bearing fruit. In the same way, when our hearts are hard and rocky, we can not bear fruit for the Lord. How do our hearts become hard? From sin in our lives. Scripture declares that sin separates us from God.

> Surely the arm of the LORD is not too short to save, nor His ear too dull to hear.
>
> But your iniquities have separated you from your God; your sins have hidden his face from you, so that He will not hear (Isaiah 59:1-2 NIV).

Figure 1 shows a person who is separated from God. The barrier between God and the man is sin. Notice how the barrier restricts all communication

Figure 1
Sin seperates us from the Lord.

and fellowship between them. When our sins separate us from the Lord, we are unable to hear the gentle voice of the Holy Spirit as He whispers to our hearts. When we are in this condition we have no desire to read His Word. If we try, it makes little sense to us. When we are separated like this, our prayer life is totally void of excitement because we feel we are talking to ourselves. There is no interchange. So our hearts become hardened. Our love for the Lord grows cold, and we begin to love the world more than we love God. We begin to love sin more than righteousness, and the barrier becomes larger. The sin barrier is impenetrable. We cannot remove it in our own strength. The only way for it to be removed is by God granting us repentance. This requires cooperation with God. REPENTANCE CONSISTS OF GOD DOING HIS PART, AND US DOING OUR PART.

GOD'S PART IN REPENTANCE

Figure 2 illustrates the anatomy of repentance. It shows that God starts the process of repentance by sending the Holy Spirit to bring conviction of sin. Without a supernatural intervention of God, we could never repent — nor would we care to do so. It is not in our nature. The Holy Spirit initiates the process by convicting us and making us aware of our sins.

> When He (the Holy Spirit) comes, He will convict the world of guilt in regard to sin and righteousness and judgment (John 16:8 NIV).

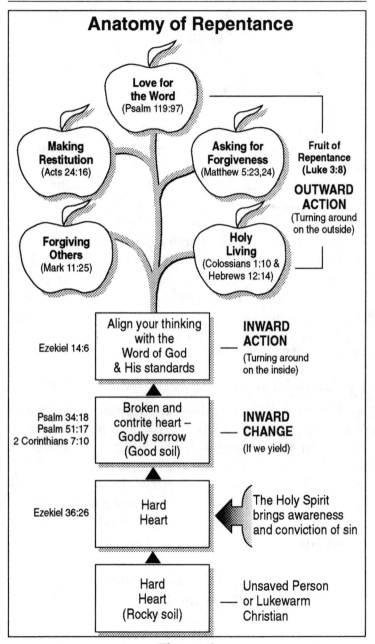

Figure 2

God is Holy and Righteous. His standard is perfect. I used to think that the commandments of God were just for lost sinners — to show them how far they fall short of God's standard of righteousness. Then one day, as I was meditating on the Ten Commandments, it became painfully clear to me that I too fall short. I realized that I need His supernatural power to live the Christian life EVERY DAY just as I needed God's supernatural power to give me new birth into the Christian life.

We can invite the Holy Spirit to make us aware of our shortcomings by reading almost anywhere in Scripture. His Word is full of descriptions of what He desires us to become. Whenever the Word instructs to do something or to act a certain way, God provides the power for us to accomplish His will. When we fail to respond, we fall short of His will for our lives. This is sin. We will discuss this in more detail in the next chapter.

GOD AND MAN WORKING TOGETHER IN REPENTANCE

God initiates the repentance process by convicting us of the sin that separates us from His presence. The light of His holiness shines upon us, and we realize how far we fall short of His righteous standard. He shows us the hardness of our hearts.

At that point the Holy Spirit attempts to break down the hardness. He does this through a process of brokenness. His desire is to produce a broken and contrite heart in us. In so doing, He breaks the hard soil of the heart, making it more receptive to

His Word. He reveals in the Word that He desires
for us to have such a heart condition.

The LORD is nigh unto them that are of a
broken heart; and saveth such as be of a
contrite spirit (Psalm 34:18 KJV).

The sacrifices of God are a broken spirit: a
broken and a contrite heart, O God, thou wilt
not despise (Psalm 51:17 KJV).

GOD'S PART is to initiate the brokenness
process, and OUR PART is to yield to Him. If we
allow Him to truly show us how much we have
offended Him by our sins, we will weep over our
sins. When we realize that every sin we have
committed helped nail Christ to the cross we will
understand the magnitude of our sin. We will
realize how much He suffered because of us as He
took the blame and punishment for our sins.
   Meditating on these things may lead to a type of
sorrow Scripture calls godly sorrow. Godly sorrow
must be distinguished from worldly sorrow.

Godly sorrow brings repentance that leads to
salvation and leaves no regret, but worldly
sorrow brings death (2 Corinthians 7:10 NIV).

Just being sorry is not repentance. Every one
who gets caught doing something wrong is sorry
they got caught. I believe godly sorrow relates to a
broken and contrite heart. Here are some examples
from Scripture:

In bitterness of soul Hannah wept much and prayed to the LORD (1 Samuel 1:10 NIV).

"Remember, O LORD, how I have walked before you faithfully and with wholehearted devotion and have done what is good in your eyes." And Hezekiah wept bitterly (2 Kings 20:3 NIV).

While Ezra was praying and confessing, weeping and throwing himself down before the house of God, a large crowd of Israelite — men, women and children — gathered around him. They too wept bitterly (Ezekiel 10:1 NIV).

I have been told that this kind of brokenness and agonizing prayer was widespread during the revivals of Jonathan Edwards and Charles Finney. So we can see that a broken and contrite heart is the result of our cooperating with God as He convicts us of our sins.

INWARD ACTIONS ASSOCIATED WITH REPENTANCE.

This part of the repentance process is turning from sin to God. A person who loves his sin stands facing the sin with his back to God. To repent is to literally turn your back on sin and look toward God. It consists of aligning our thinking and our attitudes with the Word of God and His standards. It involves renouncing behaviors that we know are contrary to the Word and will of God. The Spirit of God put it this way when He spoke through Ezekiel:

Therefore say to the house of Israel, "This is what the Sovereign LORD says: Repent! Turn from your idols and renounce all your detestable practices!" (Ezekiel 14:6 NIV).

This is an inward change of heart and attitude. It involves developing a love for the Lord and a hatred for the sins we used to enjoy. Scripture says,

Ye that love the LORD, hate evil (Psalm 97:10 KJV).

Scripture also tells us that this hatred of evil comes from reading the Word of God.

Through thy precepts I get understanding; therefore I hate every false way (Psalm 119:104 KJV).

OUTWARD ACTIONS ASSOCIATED WITH REPENTANCE:

John the Baptist spoke of outward actions associated with repentance in Luke 3:8, saying

Produce fruit in keeping with repentance. And do not begin to say to yourselves, "We have Abraham as our father." For I tell you that out of these stones God can raise up children for Abraham (Luke 3:8 NIV).

Even though God is our Father, we must understand that daily repentance is still necessary to maintain our relationship with Him. If true repentance is present, there will be fruits in keeping

with that repentance. The repentance will be
evident in our lives.

While aligning our thinking and attitudes with
the Word of God can be considered an inward
turning around, bringing forth the fruits of
repentance is an outward turning around. The
following five fruits (outward actions) of
repentance are essential for breaking down that
barrier that separates us from God and from others.
But the outward actions must spring forth as a
result of an inward change. Just going through the
motions of outward actions is not repentance.

THE FRUIT OF REPENTANCE

1. MAKING RESTITUTION
Sometimes it is possible to return something we
have stolen or pay back money we have taken.
Recently I shared with a high school evangelism
team about the need for making restitution when
the Holy Spirit convicts us. I told them that as I
read Proverbs I was reminded by the Holy Spirit
that, as a youngster, I used to steal from my parents.
Proverbs 28:24 pierced my heart as I read,

> He who robs his father or mother and says,
> "It's not wrong," he is a partner to him who
> destroys (Proverbs 28:24 NIV).

I told the kids that I felt led to send a letter
asking for forgiveness. I also enclosed an amount
of money that I thought would cover the theft.
After the meeting, one of the students confessed
that she had done the same thing when she was

younger. She said she was determined to make restitution immediately. She paid her Dad back $200.00 from her part-time job earnings. Making restitution is a frightening and difficult thing to do because one never knows what the person might think of you when you confess to them. But after it has been done, joy (and relief) floods the soul.

> So I strive always to keep my conscience clear before God and man (Acts 24:16 NIV).

2. ASKING FORGIVENESS
Scripture seems to indicate that asking forgiveness is more important than coming to the Lord in prayer.

> Therefore, if you are offering your gift at the altar and there remember that your brother has something against you, leave your gift there in front of the altar. First go and be reconciled to your brother; then come and offer your gift (Matt 5:23-24 NIV).

This is probably true because after the matter is settled the Lord will hear our prayers.

It has been said that the great missionary to China, Jonathan Goforth, was having a difficult season of preaching when the Holy Spirit convicted him that a fellow missionary had something against him. While he preached, the Holy Spirit spoke to his spirit saying, "You hypocrite! You know you do not really love your brother. If you do not straighten this thing out, I cannot bless you." So Jonathan Goforth immediately prayed, "Lord, just as soon as this meeting is over, I'll go and set this matter straight." Immediately following that prayer the power of God surged through the meeting and many in attendance broke down in tears of repentance. Unprecedented spiritual awakening and revival followed.

3. FORGIVING

I discussed a situation in my book, *A Personal Relationship*, that deals with forgiving others. I had become angry and bitter about a computer system I purchased from a Christian brother. The system did not work as it was supposed to work. After two years of tinkering on the project, all I had was a very expensive word processor. My anger and bitterness hindered my relationship with the Lord.

Then one day the Holy Spirit convicted me that I needed to forgive this man and release him. I wrote a letter to him expressing my forgiveness. The freedom and relief I felt helped me to realize that writing the letter did more for me than it did for him. Scripture says that not forgiving someone can also interfere with our prayers.

> And when you stand praying, if you hold anything against anyone, forgive him, so that your Father in heaven may forgive you your sins (Mark 11:25 NIV).

Are there people you avoid because they offended you in some way? Are there businesses you no longer go to because someone there treated you wrong? Is holding a grudge worth more than an effective prayer life?

And, by the way, when someone comes to you asking for your forgiveness, please do not say something like this, "Oh it is all right. You do not need to be sorry about that."

Instead, graciously accept the apology and verbally express your forgiveness. It is hard enough to ask someone for forgiveness. Do not make it any more difficult for the person who is doing it by refusing to accept it. If the Holy Spirit is convicting them to do it, let them do it.

4. HOLY LIVING, BY GOD'S POWER

> Make every effort to live in peace with all men and to be holy; without holiness no one will see the Lord (Hebrews 12:14 NIV).

> And we pray this in order that you may live a life worthy of the Lord and may please him in every way: bearing fruit in every good work, growing in the knowledge of God (Colossians 1:10 NIV).

None of us live a life that does not influence others. We are all leaders because we lead people to either heaven or hell. We are all salespersons because we either sell people on righteousness or unrighteousness. We are all examples of either right living or wrong living. People watch us and follow our lead. There is no neutral ground. Our actions show people that we are either for Jesus or against Him.

God calls His children to holiness. Christ is holy and we are to be conformed into His image. And a holy life will be a light and a positive influence to those around us. Holiness is impossible without the daily empowering of the Holy Spirit. We must desire to live a holy life because it honors God. Yet we must realize that we can approach that goal only through the strength that is in Christ. We must love holiness and pursue holiness. One way to love holiness is to develop a hatred for sin. When the Holy Spirit convicts us of a sin, we must not simply feel sorry because we committed a sin or that we got caught, because maybe we still have a love for that sin. Ask the Lord to show you the consequences of that particular sin in your life and in the lives of others. For when we see how sin can effect people we will begin to despise it in our lives.

For example, loving the world more than we love God can lead others to believe that Jesus is not very important. If they see that we do not put Him first in our lives why should they put Him first? This could lead them to never come to repentance and therefore perish in hell.

Figure 3 illustrates that we are capable of leading our friends, relatives and others to their destruction. Our life will either influence them to take the narrow path that leads to life or the wide path that leads to destruction.

We have been called to rescue people with the Gospel message, but sometimes our lives direct them to their destruction. None of us would knowingly lead a person to his destruction, yet sometimes, by our lives, we do it.

Figure 3
The way we live may
lead others to their destruction.

Proverbs 24:11,12 (NIV) says,

Rescue those being led away to death; Hold back those staggering toward the slaughter. If you say, "But we knew nothing about this," does not he who weighs the heart perceive it? Does not he who guards your life know it? Will he not repay each person according to what he has done?

The way we live is important because the things we do speak louder than the things we say. And the way we think effects what we do and say. The types of books we read, the type of music we listen to and the movies we watch all influence our thinking. Do the books and music and movies we expose ourselves to glorify God? Do they draw us closer to Him, or do they pull us away from Him?

Another example of how our thoughts and actions can harmfully affect people could include lustful thoughts. Thoughts can lead to sexual sin. Think of the possible effects. Men, the young lady you involve may be a weak Christian unable to withstand temptation. Sexual sin could lead to the shipwrecking of her faith, guilt and depression possibly to the point of suicide. And young women need to be aware that the way they cover themselves with clothes (or not cover themselves) and the way they act can lead young men astray in their thoughts and actions.

5. LOVE FOR THE WORD
Another fruit of repentance is a love for the Word of God. Not just reading the Word but obeying what it says. James says,

Do not merely listen to the word, and so
deceive yourselves. Do what it says (James
1:22 NIV).

A life of obedience can be summed up in one
sentence: HEARING THE WORD OF GOD AND
OBEYING IT. And how can we hear what the Word
of God says if we do not read it. And what better
time to read the Word than when our hearts have
been broken and softened by the LORD? When the
sin barrier is removed, through repentance, our
hearts become fertile soil— soil that is receptive to
the seeds of His Word.

Four

Holy Spirit, Convict Me

If we are open to the conviction of the Holy Spirit, He will make us aware of where we fall short of God's standard. While reading the Word of God, the Holy Spirit can convict us if we are receptive. Another way of exposing ourselves to the conviction of the Spirit is by reading the Ten Commandments, as found in Exodus chapter 20. We must remember that trying to follow the Ten Commandments cannot save any one. The law of God was designed to show us how sinful we are. It was designed to show us how helpless we are without Him. The Law shows us how much we need His help every day.

Here are the Ten Commandments. Let us see how we measure up to this Standard.

Thou shalt have no other gods before Me.

This means that we are to love God with everything we have and with everything we are. Jesus put it this way:

> And thou shalt love the Lord thy God with all thy heart, and with all thy soul, and with all

thy mind, and with all thy strength: this is the
first commandment (Mark 12:30).

That love is to be so intense that love for your
family seems like hate in comparison. If we love
anything or anyone more than we love God, we are
guilty of breaking this law. Money can become a
god. A house can become a god. A car can become
a god. A person we admire can become a god.

One way to violate this law is to refuse to
acknowledge God in our everyday decisions.
When we try to be the boss in our own lives we are
acting as though we are God. There is a throne
deep within each of us. It is a place the Lord has
reserved for himself. It is a very intimate place. He
is THAT concerned for us to want to be THAT close
to us so that He can be with us and help us through
everything we face in this life. And when we
choose to sit on that throne, we are doing the same
thing Lucifer did when he said, "I will be like the
most high" (Isaiah 14:14). Every time we try to run
our lives without God's loving guidance, we are
acting like we are God.

It is a foolish and dangerous thing to kick God
off the throne in our lives. Can we stand in the
shoes of the King of Kings? Can we fill the job
description of the Almighty? Can we handle our
responsibilities plus His responsibilities?

If we have ever kicked God off the throne of our
lives we have violated this first law of God.

Thou shalt not make unto thee any graven image, or likeness . . . thou shalt not bow down thyself to them, nor serve them.

In Old Testament times, men constructed graven images (such as goats, cows, birds, fish, etc.). Today we are not so obvious, as the ancient idolators, to worship statues or idols. Evangelist Ray Comfort points out that we do make images of God in our own minds. The Bible says God created man in His own image. But if we do not like what God says, we try to make God in our image. In other words, we create in our minds the kind of god that makes us feel comfortable. We do this whenever we say things about God that are not true, things that are not accurate to His Holy Word. Things like, "God would not create a hell," or "God is a God of love. He does not get angry." When we misrepresent God or twist what He said, in any way, we are fortifying this new image of God we have created in our own mind.

I understand that in India there are millions of gods. That could be likened to a religious smorgasbord. If you do not like this god then try that god. One could go god-hopping until he found a god he is comfortable with. But if we do not accept God for what He is and who He is, and if we create some other image of Him in our minds, we are guilty of idolatry, and we have broken this law.

Thou shalt not take the name of the Lord thy God in vain; for the Lord will not hold him guiltless that taketh His name in vain.

Jesus declared:

But I say unto you, That every idle word that
men shall speak, they shall give account thereof
in the day of judgment (Matthew 12:36).

Taking the name of the Lord in vain is a very
serious matter. Imagine for a moment you lived in
a land that was ruled by a great king. Now, this
king is looked up to by everyone because he is fair
and honest and because he protects his people.
Imagine that this king has a most prized possession
— a beautiful and priceless crystal set. A set that is
so priceless it is only used on the most special of
occasions.

Now imagine a farmer stealing one of those
crystal cups and using it to shovel manure in his
barn. That is very similar to taking the name of the
LORD in vain, because when we do, we speak the
name of Him who is called: Wonderful, Counselor,
Prince of Peace, Everlasting Father, Mighty God,
King of Kings, Lord of Lords, and the Lamb of God.
To use any one of His names as a gutter word —
mixed with four-letter words that spews like
sewerage out of our mouth when we are angry with
someone — is a horrendous violation of this law.

Remember the Sabbath Day, to keep it holy.
Do you ever set aside one day in seven to honor
God? Even He rested. He understood that in our
busy, hectic lives we would need time to rest and
time to consider what He has done for us. When
we refuse to slow down and take a day to rest and
honor God, we violate this law. If we have ever
gone more than seven days without resting and
honoring God, we have broken this law.

Honor thy father and thy mother: that thy days may be long upon the land.
Honor means to "value or to show respect for."
The Word says,

> Children, obey your parents in the Lord: for this is right. Honor your father and mother (which is the first commandment with promise). That it may be well with thee, and that thou mayest live long on the earth (Ephesians 6:1-3 NIV).

The promise that children will live long on the earth is not a promise of idle words. Deuteronomy 21:18 records that in Old Testament times STUBBORN or REBELLIOUS children actually received the death penalty. Therefore, if we ever have been stubborn or rebellious with our parents, we have broken this law.

Thou shalt not kill.
You may be saying, "Oh, finally we got to a law that I haven't broken!" So you haven't murdered anyone. That's good. I hope you never do. But listen to the deeper interpretation of this law through the words of Scripture:

> Whosoever hates his brother is a murderer: and ye know that no murderer has eternal life abiding in him (1 John 3:15).

The Old Testament dealt with outward actions, such as actually killing someone. But the New Testament deals with INWARD motives and the

fiery emotions that take hold of us. Jesus explained
it this way:

> You have heard that it was said by them of old,
> "Thou shalt not kill; and whosoever shall kill
> shall be in danger of the judgment." But I say
> unto you, "That whosoever is angry with his
> brother without a cause shall be in danger of
> the judgment" (Matthew 5:21-22a).

So we see, in the eyes of God, hatred, anger and
name-calling are as bad as actually killing a person.
But you may say, "How can God know if I am
angry or bitter at someone?" Some of His abilities
are revealed in Ecclesiastes 12:14:

> For God shall bring every work into judgment,
> with every secret thing, whether it be good or
> whether it be evil.

And Proverbs 5:21 says, "For the ways of a man
are before the eyes of the Lord."
So if we have ever killed or harbored anger or
bitterness or hatred, we have violated this law.

Thou shalt not commit adultery.
Again with this commandment, God looks on
our hearts — on our hidden and secret desires.
Jesus said,

> I say unto you, that whosoever looketh on a
> woman to lust after her hath committed
> adultery already with her in his heart (Matthew
> 5:28).

Our hearts are laid bare before the Lord. We can keep no secrets from Him. Psalm 44:21 declares:

Shall not God search this out? for He knoweth the secrets of the heart.

The inclination of our hearts is toward evil, if we are not walking in the Spirit. And our hearts specialize in deceiving us into believing that our impure thoughts are alright. Jeremiah declares,

The heart is deceitful above all things, and desperately wicked: who can know it? I the LORD search the heart. I try the reins, even to give every man according to his ways and according to the fruit of his doings (Jeremiah 17:9-10).

It is clear that He knows the thoughts of our hearts, and it is clear that we will stand accountable every idle thought. Yes, adultery (even in our thoughts) is a violation of this law. And by the way, this law includes any sexual encounter with anyone other than the one you are married to. It includes incest, homosexuality, beastiality etc. Being involved in any of these sexual sins, in thought or action, is a violation of this law.

Thou shalt not steal.
The Bible says, "No thief shall inherit the kingdom of God." Do we steal? Or do we change the word from steal to appropriate or borrow? At work, we may take little things that don't belong to

us. It does not matter what the value of the item is. If it is not ours it is not ours to take. But we say, "Oh, everybody does it." But does that make it right?

Yet I know that there are a lot of honest employees who have never stolen from their employers. Let us say that you are one of them. But have you ever failed to do something for someone in need when God prompts you? When this happens we are, in effect, stealing from them what God wants to give them through us. This places a whole new light on the word stealing. We can steal time from our wife and children. And we can steal time from God. We can steal from our relatives, neighbors and friends.

For example, one day a retired physical therapist came to my office. After visiting with him about physical therapy, the profession we shared, the man left. Later that day, I found myself weeping for that man as I thought about him. I did not fully understand what was happening at the time, but I felt I should talk with him about the condition of his soul. I procrastinated. I did not call him. He died a few days later. I believe I was guilty of stealing from him in the worst sense of the word. I denied him of knowledge that he would have gladly given everything he owned for. So, if we have ever been involved with any type of stealing, we have violated this law.

Thou shalt not bear false witness against thy neighbor.

In modern language this means telling fibs or white lies. Have you ever stretched the truth?

When we stretch something we pull it out of shape. Have you ever made exaggerated claims about yourself in the form of boasting? Have you ever exaggerated claims about your neighbor in the form of gossip?

Exodus 23:1 commands us not to raise a "false report and not to be an unrighteousness witness." This would apply if you misrepresent anything you see or hear. Any lie, no matter how large or how small, aligns you with Satan who is called the father of lies.

John 8:44 reveals:

> There is no truth in him. When he speaks a lie, he speaks of his own: for he is a liar, and the father of it.

I think everyone would agree that it is not a wise thing to lie. If we have ever lied, exaggerated, stretched the truth or passed along gossip, we have violated this commandment and we are guilty before an all-seeing God.

Thou shalt not covet.

To covet means to be greedy or materialistic. We covet when we desire or wish we had something our neighbor has, such as his wife, his house, his car, his truck, his job or anything else he or she has.

Money is, of course, the easiest things to covet. People covet money because more and more money buys bigger and better things.

But consider this: What possession can we strive for that is more important — more valuable than our own life? Listen to what Jesus said about this:

> For what is a man profited, if he shall gain the whole world, and lose his own soul? or what shall a man give in exchange for his soul? (Mark 8:36-37).

We have just seen that the Holy Spirit can use the Commandments to convict us. He can also make us aware of sin as we read almost anywhere in the Word. Sometimes He will bring to mind a sin from years past. This might be a specific sexual sin or a specific involvement with an occult activity. When this happens, it is best to repent of the sin and renounce it.

At first I wondered why past sins come to mind from time to time. Because when we come to Christ we are washed clean by His blood. Our sins are forgiven and forgotten. Yet when we ask the Holy Spirit to convict us, He brings some of those sins to mind. Perhaps they are sins that we never specifically repented of or renounced. I believe some sins can produce strongholds in our lives. The Lord knows that we are weak in these areas. If we do not fortify ourselves against them they may overtake us again.

So when a specific sin comes to your mind do not immediately cast it off as from Satan. It might be conviction of the Holy Spirit. Confess it and renounce it and appropriate the cleansing power of the blood of Jesus. However, if the same sin continues to come to mind to haunt you and condemn you, be assured that these thoughts are not coming from God. If this happens, and you know you repented of the sin, remember that there is no condemnation to those who are in Christ.

There is therefore now no condemnation to them which are in Christ Jesus, who walk not after the flesh, but after the Spirit (Romans 8:1).

Be sure you have truly repented and then stand firm knowing the forgiveness God grants is firm. Resist the devil and he will leave you.

Conviction List

It is important to take a close look at ourselves to see if there are any unconfessed sins that may be hindering our relationship with the Lord. We can do this by asking ourselves questions. As you read, ask the Holy Spirit to convict you and make you aware of any of the following sins you have committed. You might want to use a pencil and paper to make a conviction list as the Holy Spirit convicts you of each specific sin.

- Do I love the Lord with all my heart, with all my soul, with all my mind and with all my strength?
- Is my love for Jesus so intense that my love for my family and friends seems like hate in comparison?
- Do I consider various things or activities more important than serving God?
- Do I love my neighbor as I love myself?
- Do I love my enemies?
- Have I ever made images of God, in my mind, that are not consistent with His Word?
- Have I ever tried to twist His Word to fit my ideas?

- Have I ever accused God of being a liar by not believing what He has said in His Word?
- Have I ever taken His holy name in vain?
- Have I always honored my father and mother?
- Have I ever murdered or committed variations of murder by hating, backbiting or spreading gossip about someone?
- Do I ever entertain thoughts that I would not want everyone to know about?
- Do I ever go places that I would not want my pastor to know about?
- Does the music I listen to glorify God?
- Do the movies I watch honor God?
- Have I ever looked at pornographic materials?
- Have I ever taken part in an occult activity such as astrology, witchcraft, Ouija Board, palm reading etc.?
- Have I ever stolen without making restitution?
- Do I lie, exaggerate, or stretch the truth?
- Do I covet things that do not belong to me?
- Am I envious of gifts, abilities, or qualities others have?
- Have I ever wronged someone without making it right?
- Have I withheld forgiveness from anyone who has wronged me?
- Do I harbor anger or bitterness?
- As a husband, do I love my wife as Christ loved the Church?
- As a wife, do I love and honor my husband?
- Am I guilty of pride?

- Am I ever selfish?
- Do I have a love for the lost ones that Jesus died for?
- Am I all that I can be for God?

If we have sinned against a person, Scripture encourages us to go to them.

Therefore confess your sins to each other and pray for each other so that you may be healed (James 5:16 NIV).

You might approach them saying something like this: "The Holy Spirit has convicted me and made me aware that I have sinned against you in this way. I am very sorry and I am asking you to forgive me."

If we have sinned against God, ask Him for forgiveness. A suggested prayer could be something like the following:

"Lord you have shown me that I have sinned against you in the following way . . . . I turn from that activity. I renounce that activity or behavior. I know that my sinful behavior helped to nail Jesus to the cross. And I am truly sorry. I ask for your forgiveness, knowing that You always stand ready to forgive. Cleanse me by the precious blood of Jesus so that I can be clean in your presence. And empower me by your Holy Spirit to resist those sins in the future. I ask this in the mighty name of Jesus, Amen."

1 John 1:8-10 summarizes our condition and God's remedy.

If we say we have no sin, we deceive ourselves, and the truth is not in us. If we confess our sins, he is faithful and just to forgive us our sins, and to cleanse us from all unrighteousness. If we say that we have not sinned, we make him a liar, and His word is not in us.

Six

Anatomy of Our "First Love"

Exactly what did Jesus mean by "first love" when He spoke of it to the Christians at the church in Ephesus? He said,

> Yet I hold this against you: You have forsaken your first love.
>
> Remember the height from which you have fallen! Repent and do the things you did at first. If you do not repent, I will come to you and remove your lampstand from its place (Revelation 2:4-5 NIV).

Scripture shows us the progression of the "first love" experience in Acts 3:19.

> Repent ye therefore, and be converted, that your sins may be blotted out, when the times of refreshing shall come from the presence of the Lord (Acts 3:19 KJV).

Figure 4 illustrates the components of Acts 3:19 as follows:

First Love

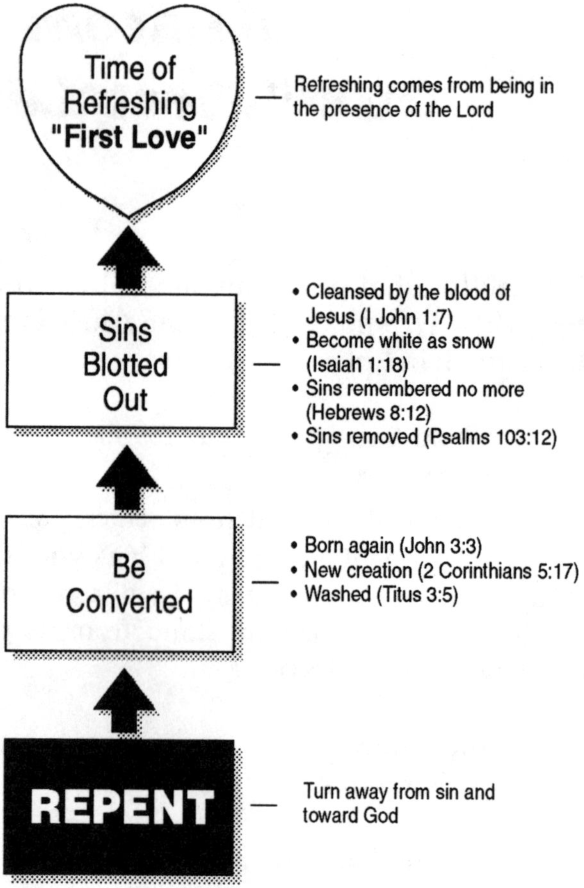

Time of
Refreshing
"First Love"

— Refreshing comes from being in
the presence of the Lord

**Sins
Blotted
Out**

— • Cleansed by the blood of
Jesus (I John 1:7)
• Become white as snow
(Isaiah 1:18)
• Sins remembered no more
(Hebrews 8:12)
• Sins removed (Psalms 103:12)

**Be
Converted**

— • Born again (John 3:3)
• New creation (2 Corinthians 5:17)
• Washed (Titus 3:5)

REPENT

— Turn away from sin and
toward God

"Repent ye therefore, and **be converted**, that
your **sins** may be **blotted out**, when the **times
of refreshing** shall come from the presence of
the Lord." Acts 3:19

Figure 4

A. REPENT: A sinner turns to God for the very first time. He turns away from sin and brings forth the inward and outward changes associated with repentance.

B. BE CONVERTED: The repentant sinner trusts in the finished work of Christ. He believes that he has sinned greatly and has an impossible debt to pay. He knows that Jesus loved him so much that He chose to come to earth as a man and stand in his place — to take the blame and punishment for his sins. Jesus spoke of this conversion experience to Nicodemus.

> Verily, verily, I say unto thee, "Except a man be born again, he cannot see the kingdom of God" (John 3:3 KJV).

Scripture makes it very clear that a sinner cannot earn his salvation by being good enough or by doing any number of good works.

> Not by works of righteousness which we have done, but according to His mercy He saved us, by the washing of regeneration, and renewing of the Holy Ghost (Titus 3:5 KJV).

True conversion produces an inward change. The sinner becomes a new person with new desires and new attitudes.

> Therefore if any man be in Christ, he is a new creature: old things are passed away; behold, all things are become new (2 Corinthians 5:17 KJV).

C. SINS ARE BLOTTED OUT (erased): At this
time, the entire sin debt of the individual is
removed and he stands free from the mountain of
guilt for the first time in his life. Scripture says
much about how our sins are blotted out.

> But if we walk in the light, as He is in the light,
> we have fellowship with one another, and the
> blood of Jesus, His Son, purifies us from all sin
> (1 John 1:7 NIV).

> "Come now, let us reason together," says the
> LORD. "Though your sins are like scarlet, they
> shall be as white as snow; though they are red
> as crimson, they shall be like wool" (Isaiah 1:18
> NIV).

> For I will forgive their wickedness and will
> remember their sins no more (Hebrews 8:12
> NIV).

> As far as the east is from the west, so far has He
> removed our transgressions from us (Psalm
> 103:12 NIV).

D. TIME OF REFRESHING: This time of
refreshing comes from being in the presence of the
Lord for the first time. Until this moment sin has
created a wall between the sinner and God. Now
that the sin is removed, the new Christian can enter
into His presence — a place that is always
refreshing. And think of the fact that all sin and
guilt is absent for the first time. The person
becomes overwhelmed with joy. When he

considers that God would provide such a plan, gratitude fills his soul. THIS IS THE FIRST LOVE.

I feel that daily repentance can bring all Christians into the presence of the Lord. They will experience the "time of refreshing," as a result of their daily cleansing from sin. I would like to think that we could learn to live in the fullness of that "first love" condition, but I think that daily cleansing can never compare with that initial washing we experience when we first become a member of the family of God. But I think we can approach the magnitude of joy and refreshing of that first love condition by developing a repentant heart.

There is an important distinction to be made before we leave Acts 3:19. Notice the progression of the verse: repentance...conversion...sins washed away...followed by a time of refreshing. I used to violate this progression when I "led people to the Lord." I did not talk a lot about sin and the need for repentance. Instead, I promised them that God had a wonderful plan for their lives. I told them that Jesus offers them peace, joy, happiness and a better life. I told them that God loves them and wants to bless them more than they can ever imagine. The sad thing about this is that all of the above things are TRUE. However, these benefits of salvation are only secondary. Each of us must come to God on His terms and come to salvation under His conditions.

Scripture says that Jesus came into the world to save sinners (1 Timothy 1:15). The Word also instructs us that the method of calling sinners is through repentance.

I CAME not TO CALL the righteous, but
SINNERS TO REPENTANCE (Mark 2:17).

And again Jesus said that,

REPENTANCE and REMISSION OF SINS
should be preached . . . (Luke 24:47).

So when we invite a person to come to Jesus by
offering them the benefits of salvation without
telling them the need for repentance, we deceive
them into thinking they are converted, washed and
saved. But in reality many of them could wake up
someday in hell because they never came to God on
His terms.

Sinners need to know that each of us has
violated God's laws. Each of us stands on death
row awaiting our sentence of death because "the
wages of sin is death (Romans 6:23). They need to
know that God loved us so much that He sent Jesus
to come to suffer and die in our place. Jesus came
to take the blame for all the rotten things we have
ever done — all the sins we ever committed. They
need to know that true salvation comes only from
acknowledging our sinful condition and throwing
ourselves at God's feet, in repentance, asking for
His mercy, His grace and His forgiveness. It would
be well for each of us who names the name of
Christ to think back to our own conversion
experience and determine whether we entered
through the door of true repentance.

Seven

The Repentant Heart and Evangelism

Another product of a repentant heart is more effective evangelism.

Psalm 51 reveals an important key to effective evangelism. Listen to a summary of the verses. Watch the progression:

vs   1 Have mercy on me
       Blot out my transgressions
vs   2 Wash me; cleanse me
vs   3 For I am conscious of my sin
vs   4 I have sinned against you
vs   7 Purify me
vs   8 Make me hear joy and gladness
vs 10 Create in me a clean heart
vs 11 Cast me not away from your presence
vs 12 Restore to me the joy of my salvation
vs. 13 THEN will I teach transgressors your ways, and sinners shall be converted and return to You.

Notice that a cry for mercy came first. This heartfelt cry is followed by the cleansing of sins and the creation of a pure heart. Being cleansed from sin leads to that joyful time of refreshing where one experiences the joy of his salvation. When a person's heart is cleansed, made pure and filled with joy, he has something to offer to a lost world.

Jesus commanded us to preach the message of repentance and remission of sins (Luke 24:47). It only makes sense that if we practice daily repentance, sharing that message will me more effective.

But before we evangelize, we must ask God to prepare the way. We must talk to God about men before we talk to men about God.

E.M. Bounds said it this way, "Talking to men for God is a great thing, but talking to God for men is greater still. He will never talk well and with real success to men for God who has not learned well how to talk to God for men" (*Power Through Prayer*, pg 27).

We will find, as we pray for the lost, that the Lord will sometimes share His heartfelt longings with us. When this happens, we find ourselves weeping for the lost because of their hopeless, sinful condition. We become grieved when we realize that many of those Christ shed His blood for will perish in hell if they do not turn to Him. When we weep and pray for the lost before we go to them, we can understand the meaning of Psalm 126:5-6,

> They that sow in tears shall reap in joy. He that goeth forth and weepeth, bearing precious seed, shall doubtless come again with rejoicing, bringing his sheaves with him.

Other Benefits of having a Repentant Heart

Since repentance is the foundation of a repentant heart, these terms will be used interchangeable in the following list:

1. A repentant heart makes our prayers more effective.

> Because your heart was tender and penitent and you humbled yourself before God when you heard His words against this place and its inhabitants, and humbled yourself before Me and rent your clothes and wept before Me, I have heard you , says the Lord (2 Chronicles 34:27) Amplified version.

2. Repentance produces joy in heaven.

> Likewise, I say unto you, there is joy in the presence of the angels of God over one sinner that repenteth (Luke 15:10 KJV).

3. Repentance helps us to acknowledge the truth that sets us free from the snares of the devil.

And the Lord's servant must not quarrel;
instead, he must be kind to everyone, able to
teach, not resentful.

Those who oppose him he must gently instruct,
in the hope that God will grant them
repentance leading them to a knowledge of the
truth.

And that they will come to their senses and
escape from the trap of the devil, who has
taken them captive to do his will (2 Timothy
2:24-26 NIV).

4. A repentant heart is esteemed by God.

This is the one I esteem: he who is humble and
contrite [repentant] in spirit, and trembles at
my word (Isaiah 66:2).

5. God revives those with repentant hearts. A
repentant heart is a humble and contrite heart.

For thus saith the high and lofty One that
inhabiteth eternity, whose name is Holy; I
dwell in the high and holy place, with him also
that is of a contrite and humble spirit, to revive
the spirit of the humble, and to REVIVE the
heart of the contrite [repentant] ones (Isaiah
57:15 KJV).

A dictionary definition of the word "revive" is:
1) To restore to consciousness or life; 2) to restore
from a depressed, inactive, or unused state: bring
back; and 3) to renew in the mind or memory.

How to Develop a Repentant Heart

1 Ask God daily for a repentant heart: a broken and contrite heart. We can not repent or develop a repentant heart without His help.

2. Ask the Holy Spirit to convict you of your sins. Realize the enormity of your sins and realize that each sin helped nail Jesus to the cross.

3. Realize that with each sin, you hurt or offended God or another person.

4. Be willing to make restitution if needed.

5. Be willing to ask for forgiveness from people you have wronged or offended.

6. Be willing to forgive others for their offenses to you.

7. Be willing to allow God to change your heart, mind, attitude and actions toward sin. Realize what sin does to you and others. Ask God for a hatred of sin.

8. Weep before the Lord because of your sin. Ask for cleansing.

9. Then appropriate the cleansing power of the Blood of Jesus and realize that it washes you from each sin.

10. Realize that we were not able to become Christians without His supernatural enabling power. Neither can we walk the Christian life without that mighty power. Rely upon Him to help you through each day.

Ten

Conclusion

Will the much-needed wave of revival break forth upon our land? Only if a wave of true repentance comes first. For God can not use hard unrepentant hearts. Remember, Scripture says He REVIVES those who are repentant (Isaiah 57:15).

I believe the Father longs to create in us repentant hearts — hearts that are sensitive and responsive to His will — hearts that will no longer tolerate sin in their lives. For those with repentant hearts understand that we fall so short of God's righteous standard. Repentant hearts realize that sin separates us from God and from others. And they realize that true repentance with brokenness of heart can remove all the barriers that separate us from God and others.

CLOSING PRAYER

O Lord, I uplift your church, Your Bride. Revive us, O God. In many countries Your people are dying for You. But in America we can hardly live for You. We have sought after power and prosperity and success instead of seeking after You.

We pursue happiness rather than holiness. Forgive us for falling so short of what You desire for us. Forgive us for not allowing You to empower us to do exploits for You. Forgive us for not allowing You to impart to us Your compassion and Your love for a lost and dying world. Forgive us for our apathy and lukewarmness. Forgive us for our love for the world — that love that makes us Your enemies. Replace that love for the world with the love of the Father. O God, help us to begin every day in an attitude of repentance. Give us repentant hearts, O God. Give us hearts that acknowledge our sins and our offenses. Holy Spirit, convict us and show us how far we fall short of the Holy and Righteous standard of God. Then help us to appropriate the cleansing power of the Blood of Jesus so that we may stand clean in your presence. Then empower us, by your Spirit, so that we can rise up and become the salt and the light and the witnesses You long for us to be. Make us strong with Your strength so that we can do the work you have called us to do while there is still time.

A HARVEST PROMISE

One morning, during an intense time of agonizing prayer, I felt impressed that the Holy Spirit was saying the following to my heart:

"I am about to bring forth the spark of revival in the hearts of those who are ready. That spark shall kindle in their hearts and shall set fire to their souls. The flame of revival shall come forth in those hearts. The flame of revival shall burn the hay and stubble from their lives. It shall consume all that is not holy and righteous and shall leave only those things that are of Me, says the Lord. Wake up my people! Arise and come forth. Recognize your sin for I have come to cleanse you. Come to Me with repentant hearts and I will show you the depths of your sin but also the heights of My mercy and My grace. Repent! Turn around! Turn around, My people. Turn from your sins and return to Me and I will restore you to the heights from which you have fallen. Then you shall experience the flame of revival in your hearts and it shall spread from one to another...to another...to another...until My church is ablaze with the fire of revival. Then shall sinners come. They will be drawn by My righteousness and My holiness. And My glory shall draw them. They shall hunger and thirst after Me and they shall come, says the Lord of the Harvest."

> If My people, which are called by My name, shall humble themselves, and pray, and seek My face, and turn from their wicked ways [repent]; then will I hear from heaven, and will forgive their sin, and will heal their land (2 Chronicles 7:14).

Has the message in *Lord Give Me a Repentant Heart* ministered to you in some way? Has it given you hope for revival in our land? If it has and you feel there is still time for our country to turn back to God, you might consider sharing this booklet with a friend. Pastors might wish to get a copy into the hands of the members of their congregations. For this reason we are providing volume discounts as follows:

VOLUME DISCOUNTS
(We pay shipping)

1-10 copies $3.95 ea. Please order through your local Christian bookstore

11-30 copies $3.50 ea, from this publisher

31-100 copies $3.00 ea, from this publisher

101-500 copies $2.50 ea, from this publisher

501 or more copies $2.00 ea, from this publisher

ALL ORDERS MUST BE PRE-PAID
(Check or money order is accepted.)

Solid Rock Books, Inc.
979 Young Street, Suite E
Woodburn, Oregon 97071
(503)981-0705

The following pages
list additional publications
from
Solid RockBooks
for your Spiritual Growth —

*Available at fine Christian
booksellers everywhere*

Personal Relationship
by Thomas LeBlanc
Author of *Lord Give Me a Repentant Heart*

ISBN 187-911-2086

Christianity is not a religion, but a relationship – a living personal relationship with God. He desires to be a real part of our lives. He longs to develop a personal relationship with each of us.

In this book, you will read about many examples of how Jesus can touch and influence a person's life. You will see that only He can eliminate our guilt and fill our emptiness. Learn how through Him, we can overcome fear. You will understand that He offers a peace that surpasses human comprehension.

In this book you will:
- Learn how "emptiness" is filled
- See how to combat fear
- Understand God's peace
- Recognize God's faithfulness
- Discover the ingredients for a miracle

New Discovery:
- Learn how our thoughts and words affect our physical bodies.

Thomas LeBlanc is a Christian businessman, a registered physical therapist and a publisher. He has authored Christian tracts, a physical therapy article, and an electronic communications text that is used in technical colleges across the country. He lives with his wife, Karen, and three children, in Oregon.

Available from
Fine Christian Booksellers everywhere

We've Come This Far By Faith
by Carolyn Wilde
ISBN 187-911-206X

Paul and Carolyn were deeply in debt when an automobile accident led Paul to make a life-changing commitment to put God first in his life, and their extraordinary, living-by-faith adventure began.

We've Come This Far By Faith is a heart-warming book, not just about a family who learned to trust their God for their needs, but about a living, faithful, loving God who cares for His children.

We've Come This Far By Faith will challenge and inspire you to trust God to guide and take care of you as you put His principles into action in your life. The comment most often heard from readers of We've Come This Far By Faith is, *"I stayed up all night reading this book! I just couldn't put it down!"*

We've Come This Far By Faith will give you that extra faith you need to step out on the sea of life with your eyes and faith firmly fixed on Jesus Christ! He will not let His followers sink, no matter how the storms around us rage!

Available from
Fine Christian Booksellers everywhere

Seven Biblical Principles for Financial Peace of Mind

by Paul and Carolyn Wilde
ISBN 187-911-2094

How many people do you know who have financial peace of mind? Do you have it?

The number one cause of divorce today is fighting about money! MONEY!

Worrying about it causes ulcers, migraines, divorces, murders, thefts, prostitution, suicides . . . the list could go on and on, but God's Word sums it all up by saying our love for it is the root of all evil.

Did you know there are seven principles we must follow if we want the blessing of God upon our lives?

You may follow two or three of them – but do you know and follow all seven?

We, as Christians, especially in the coming days of financial turmoil and economic collapse of the monetary system as we know it, need to know and put into practice every single one of these principles. Then, and only then, will you have financial peace of mind.

This book will show you what these seven principles are and how to practice them!

Available from
Fine Christian Booksellers everywhere

Potential *BEST SELLER!*

First printing sold out in two months!

The World's Last Dictator
by Dwight L. Kinman
ISBN 187-911-2205

There is a plan to bring America into a New World Order – the secret code phrase for a one world government. Behind this plan are powerful, global, mega forces that are on an inexorable, relentless drive to establish on planet earth a super world government by the year 2000 A.D. These forces believe they have it almost within their grasp, and they are about to make a dash to the finish line.

Dwight L Kinman examines this plan, the forces behind it, and the global events that are moving the people of the planet earth toward its implementation.

Learn the truth behind events like these that are stunning the world!

- **The New World Order** – Secret Code for the One World Government
- **The Coming Money Crash** – and How to Prepare for Crisis Days
- **America 2000** – The Secret Plan to Brainwash Every Child
- **Murder at WACO** – What the media did not reveal
- **A Million Foreign Troops** – Why are they training on American Soil?
- **The implantable Microchip** – Now in animals . . . are people next?

This book will alert you to what is happening behind the scenes. It will motivate you to do what God wants you to do – for it must be done quickly while there is still time.

Available from
Fine Christian Booksellers everywhere

"For Many Shall Come In My Name"

How mainstream America is accepting the "Ancient Wisdom" teaching and what this foreshadows.

ISBN 187-911-2019

by Ray Yungen

Millions of Americans are having deep mystical experiences. As a result, the fields of teaching, healing and counseling are being profoundly affected. The very fabric of American life is being slowly transformed.

DISCOVER how popular authors such as John Bradshaw and Melody Beattie appear to be promoting ideas similar to those promoted by Shirley MacLaine; the modern-day New Age Movement in both the New and Old Testaments.

LEARN how the "centering prayer" is re-shaping some mainline denominations.

FIND OUT how some of the fastest growing techniques sweeping the medical field are based on occultism.

"Recently on television, from coast-to-coast, I made the statement that I had just read Mr. Ray Yungen's book entitled, For Many Shall Come In My Name. I added with extreme enthusiasm, that I literally experienced goose bumps while devouring its contents. Needless to say, I heartily endorse this great prophetical work and state that it is a MUST for every believer who is looking for "the Blessed Hope." – **Jack Van Impe**

Available from
Fine Christian Booksellers everywhere

A Time For WAR
Spiritual Battle Strategies for the Christian
by Pastor Frank Solberg
ISBN 187-911-2027

You Can Be Free!
  From Depression, sickness, oppression, anxiety, and despair.
  A Time for WAR is a biographical, scriptural, historical, and practical information book on dealing with unclean spirits in a non-violent method.

Section 1:
• Pastor Solberg's dealings with unclean spirits in his own life and in the churches he pastored.

Section 2:
• Spiritual warfare from a biblical perspective • The reality of unclean spirits, You Can Be Free! • Authority of the believer • Symptoms of demonic activity • Binding and loosing • Ministering angels • Weapons of warfare
• Role of spiritual gifts • Much more!

Section 3:
• Practical issues of doing battle with unclean spirits
• Counselling sessions • Preparatory prayer
• Manifestations • Model prayer of the opening session
• Model prayer to break the curse of the sins of the father • And more!

Available from
Fine Christian Booksellers everywhere

Burdens, Bruises and Bondages

by Pauline Gustafson
ISBN 187-911-2051

For those who hurt and for those who minister to the wounded, this book defines the three basic areas of need in the lives of people: Burdens, Bruises and Bondages.

For every burden, bruise and bondage, God has a remedy. The Bible records it! The Gospel includes it! The Cross secures it! Burdens are to be shared! Bruises are to be healed! Bondages are to be broken!

Available from
Fine Christian Booksellers everywhere